My Wellness Toolbox

My Wellness Toolbox

Alison Swift

Matador
9 Priory Business Park,
Wistow Road, Kibworth Beauchamp,
Leicestershire. LE8 0RX
Tel: 0116 279 2299
Email: books@troubador.co.uk
Web: www.troubador.co.uk/matador
Twitter: @matadorbooks

ISBN 978 1789014 815

British Library Cataloguing in Publication Data.
A catalogue record for this book is available from the British Library.

Printed and bound in Great Britain by 4edge Limited
Typeset in 11pt Minion Pro by Troubador Publishing Ltd, Leicester, UK

Matador is an imprint of Troubador Publishing Ltd

To Swifty.
Thank you.

CONTENTS

MY ROCK BOTTOM

One cloudy August morning in 2006, I awoke, rolled out of bed with the standard mental struggles, showered whilst worrying about the working day ahead and everything else I could think of, attempted to do my make-up without catching my own eye in the mirror, got dressed, avoided breakfast as the butterflies were working overtime, headed downstairs and tried to open the front door. I couldn't. I could neither physically nor mentally open that front door. I had hit my rock bottom.

Anxiety and panic attacks slowly absorbed my happiness over an eight(ish)-year period prior to that day. It didn't happen overnight, it wasn't sudden; during that time I didn't really know what was actually happening to me and didn't speak openly or honestly about it with anyone. I had simply got used to waking up with knots in my stomach like every day was exam day. Worrying about the journey I would take to work so trying different routes to see if there was a route that didn't make me scared. Avoiding motorways. Struggling to swallow food at meal times, so choosing food based not on what I liked but on what could be swallowed easily. Planning my escape routes from meeting rooms, shops, cinemas, public spaces, friends' homes, family's homes. Sitting with my back to people in restaurants and public places so strangers couldn't see my face. Cancelling plans because I had been physically sick at the thought of those plans. Pretending. Lying. Faking it. Smiling when inside I was breaking. Battling with my own thoughts constantly. Shouting at myself. Disliking myself.

It was no wonder that after eight years of so much negativity within my own head I had hit my rock bottom. *My rock bottom.*

"Rock bottom became the solid foundation on which I rebuilt my life."

(J. K. Rowling)

MY TOOLBOX

One sunny August morning in 2015, I awoke to the sound of my 16-month-old son calling "Mummy". I scooped him out of his cot, gave him a cuddle and handed him to Daddy to get him ready for nursery. I had a shower, took my time doing my make-up in the mirror, got dressed. As I headed for the stairs I took another look back in the full-length mirror and smiled. I grabbed some breakfast, ran out of the front door, jumped into my car and headed along the motorway to work. It was only 7.30am, yet the morning sun was already making me feel warm as it shone through to the inside of my car. I smiled. I felt lucky. I actually felt it. A song came on the radio and I immediately felt happy tears rush to my eyes. I grinned. *Crazy*. Gnarls Barkley. Just one of the many Tools in my Toolbox. My Toolbox that made me feel like me again. My Toolbox that I discovered 12 years ago and that I have been adding to ever since. My Wellness Toolbox.

I just wish that on the day I hit rock bottom, or even before then, that someone could have told me about My Wellness Toolbox. Over the years I spent so many hours obsessively searching the internet for the answers to cure me but I couldn't find anything that related to me; it was all so generic. I was never going to find the answer on the internet. There is no single answer. There is, however, a Toolbox, and it really can work. I've got mine and if you need one, want one or think you should have one (even just a little bit), then you can have one too, right now, and you can start to fill it with the tools that are useful for you.

The purpose of this book is to share the content of My Wellness Toolbox to help you start adding tools to *your* Wellness Toolbox.

I am not a doctor, a therapist, a psychologist or a medical specialist of any kind; I would never claim to be. I am just a young woman who found a way to manage and overcome anxiety, stress and depression. I want to share the tools that helped me and that are still working for me today.

Take from this anything that helps you and ignore the tools that just don't work for you. There are no right or wrong tools (unless, of course, your tools involve breaking the law – probably best to avoid these). What works for you is what is right for you!

TOOL #1
WATER

I can't actually remember the source, but I was once told that drinking water can prevent or even stop anxiety and panic attacks mid-flow. I tried it – it works – and for over 12 years one of my most-used Tools has been my trusted bottle of corporation pop.

The first warning signs of an anxiety or panic attack for me used to be light-headedness and a dry mouth. Therefore, I guess it makes sense that drinking water could immediately relieve me of the dry mouth. This then had a positive knock-on effect because the other usual suspects – pins and needles, nausea, bowels opening, trembling, and the rest – would not take hold. A few gulps and at least nine times out of ten the attack would back off.

I used to carry a bottle of water with me everywhere

or make sure I had easy access to water, ready to halt an attack if needed. It was only in recent years that I realised I had sub-conciously stopped doing this. I still make sure I have a bottle of water on hand in situations that I may feel vulnerable in or that I consider stressful. For example, job interviews, long journeys on public transport, hospital visits, hangovers. On my wedding day, 'bride's bottle of water for church' was top of the best man's checklist!

There are situations when you are not allowed to carry a bottle of water, for example, going through security at the airport. Therefore, as a substitute I always carry chewing gum or sweets when going on a flight, ideal if the dry mouth kicks in. Tickets (check). Passport (check). Money (check). Chewing Gum (check).

Once, boarding a flight with a well-known Irish budget airline, I was carrying my one piece of hand luggage and a bottle of My Wellness Toolbox water on to the flight. At the boarding gate I was advised by the gate agent that I would need to place the bottle of water in my hand luggage. I stated that this was not possible as I didn't have room and I didn't want to risk the bottle breaking and water leaking within my luggage. I was then advised that I would either need to leave the bottle of water behind or be charged for a second piece of hand luggage. I was disgusted and sadly became very anxious. That water was one of my Tools that would help me on that flight. At the time I was still very fearful in confined spaces so had come fully prepared with my Toolbox overflowing.

The panic started to rise as I was wondering at what point I would be able to get more water on the flight. I had

2

to explain to the gate agent (and a few irate passengers listening in behind me) why the water was important to me. After rolling her eyes so far back I guessed she must be looking for her empathy, she allowed me to go ahead, but with a patronising reminder: "OK, we will not charge you this time, but please remember for next time". Next time?! I now fly Aer Lingus!!

Effectiveness: 10/10. I have shared this Tool with several people over the years and they all agree water works... and as an added bonus – it keeps you hydrated!

Ease: 10/10 – unless flying with a certain low-budget Irish airline.

Budget: Free–£5

TOOL #2
BREATHE

Stop. Breathe In. Breathe Out. Give yourself a break.

The great thing about this wellness Tool is that it can be used anytime, anywhere and it doesn't cost a bean.

Breathing exercises can stop anxiety and panic attacks in their tracks, instantly reduce stress, support you during recovery of depression and can even help you sleep.

I have learned many different breathing exercises over the years. This is the one that works best for me:

Breathe in for five. Breathe out for ten.

This takes a little practice but once mastered, you will be using this exercise without realising (and without counting out loud and therefore attracting strange looks). It is very effective in making you feel calm very quickly. Try it now.

- Make sure your feet are on the ground
- Try and breathe in through your nose and out through your mouth
- Take a deep breath in and count to five
- Take a deep breath out and count to ten

It does not matter how quickly you count or for how long you do this exercise, just repeat it until you feel calmer.

This exercise is now so embedded within me I sometimes catch myself using it. It is as if my subconscious has become programmed to use it automatically in situations that would previously have made me very anxious.

Stop. Breathe. Give Yourself a Break.

When you find yourself in a stressful situation, the panic is rising and you are feeling out of control, take the following steps:

- Immediately stop what you are doing (if safe to do so)
- Breathe in for five, breathe out for ten until you start to feel calmer
- Walk away from the situation. Give yourself a break!
- Do not beat yourself up for feeling like this. Give yourself a break!
- Return to the situation when you feel calmer

I used to do this in the office environment A LOT, especially on busy days when the pressure is on, deadlines have to be met, adrenaline is pumping for all the wrong reasons, and you start to feel out of control. It is likely that this Tool has saved a few working relationships over the years… and possibly my marriage!!

You can also be proactive with this Tool, so if you can find five to ten minutes during your day, evening or bedtime to sit, relax and just breathe, then do it, and notice how good it can make you feel.

Effectiveness: 10/10. Combine Tool #1 and Tool #2 and you will really feel a difference.

Ease: 7/10. This one does require practice and some focus, but you will quickly nail it and be glad you put that effort in.

Budget: Free

TOOL #3
MUSIC – TURN IT UP

Exactly what it says on the tin. Turn up that music and blast the negativity away. Whilst you're at it, why not shake it off and have a dance-off too?!

My own thoughts were (and still can be) my worst enemy; if I sat alone for too long, a simple negative thought about something insignificant could manifest and within minutes, anxiety would be taking over. However, if I turned it on or turned it up, music could literally save me from my own thoughts.

I was once queuing in a popular high-street store waiting to make my purchase. The queue was not long but was not reducing at the speed I needed it to be. The water in my bottle was running low (i.e. a drip left), impatience was starting to kick in and I could feel the anxiety starting to dance around my ankles. I needed to get out of there. The atmosphere was still, no music was playing, and my own negative thoughts were starting to take over. I was on the verge of dumping the clothes and running when suddenly music came blasting from the speakers as if someone had suddenly realised they had forgotten to turn it on at opening time. Crazy. It was. *Crazy* by Gnarls Barkley. I breathed in and out (several times), licked the last drip of water and chuckled to myself. Did my best not to break into a dance. Paid for my goods. Left the store. Added that song to my Toolbox. Just like that.

Crazy is now on my Positive Playlist. If you have songs that uplift you, make you feel more positive or simply put a smile on your face, then create a playlist and add them all. Start each day playing your happy songs.

Effectiveness: 9/10. Music can lift you within minutes, yet sometimes you just don't feel it. That's OK.

Ease: 7/10. There are limitations as to when you can turn the music up, for example, it may not be appropriate in a quiet office or in the quiet zone of a train. If you are allowed to use earphones in the workplace, get the phone/computer set up to play your happy songs.

Budget: Free

"Dear Music, I will never be able to thank you enough for always being there for me."

(Unknown)

TOOL #4
MEDIA – TURN IT OFF

Within days of hitting my 'rock bottom', my mum convinced me to seek some help from my GP. It was time the professionals took a look, which terrified me. During the years I had been experiencing the negative thoughts and feelings, I had not really discussed (openly or honestly) any of them with anyone, especially not my doctor. I was so nervous that the answer would be drugs, which for my own personal reasons I wanted to avoid. I remember walking into the GP surgery on confession day, convinced that by the end of my appointment I would have been sectioned and locked away. How wrong I was.

My doctor was beyond supportive. During my appointment I was asked to explain when some of the worst panic attacks had happened; this helped him to understand some of the triggers that had caused the panic. Even I hadn't clocked how many of them had occurred during or shortly after reading newspapers or watching television or even talking about what was happening in the news.

The doctor told me that from that day forward, the (negative) media was to be turned off. This would mean stop reading the newspapers, stop watching the news, stop watching favourite television programmes, stop watching movies containing violence, stop indulging in all the negativity the media has to offer. I went cold turkey (as much as I realistically could) and it really did make a difference.

Tool #4 is easier said than done. There are family and friends that religiously watch the news; I would make excuses to leave the room. I stopped watching most films, dramas, documentaries, *Crimewatch*. I pretty much stopped watching TV, yet it was always the first thing my ex would automatically want to turn on when he walked in a room, and even now my husband doesn't know how to sit comfortably without a remote control in his hand watching the latest Netflix drama. Newspapers seemed to hang out everywhere, the negative headlines shouting in my face. I learned to look away, even when they were lying on the kitchen table… or bathroom floor. Men.

It was around this time social media was really taking off. I had managed to avoid Facebook for quite a while but in a moment of 'newly single – just had a glass of wine' weakness, a friend convinced me to sign up and ironically, I am now a self-confessed Facebook addict. However, I apply this Tool when needed. I automatically scroll past articles I deem negative or offensive and the filters also prove very useful for avoiding posts from the 'glass-half-empty' Facebook friends.

In recent years I have started introducing what I refer to as 'negative' media back into my life again as I now have a much more positive mindset. I am able to read the tabloids, watch documentaries… and *EastEnders*… without believing that the bad things will happen to me or my family. However, if at any time whilst reading an article or watching a film I start to over-analyse the content or it starts to make me feel the slightest bit anxious, I just TURN IT OFF or walk away. It is my choice. It is that simple.

Effectiveness: 8/10. If you can switch off then this Tool can really reduce the amount of negativity presented to you on a daily basis.

Ease: 5/10. It is easy to make the choice to switch off; however, we are all so consumed and surrounded by the media it can be very hard to ignore.

Budget: Free

TOOL #5
ESSENTIAL OILS

If you don't own an essential oil diffuser already, make sure you add one to your birthday or Christmas wish list. I received one in 2017 and not only does it look quite nice, but with the right blend of essential oils, it can make me (and my guests, without them realising why) feel good very quickly.

I've always loved an aromatherapy massage (see Tool #19) but it wasn't until I started 'playing' with essential oils and creating blends that I really appreciated the reason why there is the word 'therapy' in the title. I also realised on reflection that I hadn't appreciated the power essential oils have had on me over the years. The right blend of oils really can lift you psychologically and even improve your physical wellbeing.

It was my sister who generously bought me a set of 14 essential oils for my birthday over two years ago. They sat very politely in the box until I rediscovered them when we moved to a new house, cue the purchase of the diffuser. Since then I have done a lot of research and now I have my own catalogue of blends that I use in moments of need:

'Just annoyed on a Monday morning… just because' (normally husband-related) aka Liquid Sunshine

- 3 drops grapefruit
- 3 drops lavender
- 2 drops orange
- 2 drops peppermint

'Feeling anxious and don't know why' aka Chill Me Out

- 3 drops lavender
- 3 drops frankincense (I was surprised myself – I thought this was something from the Nativity)
- 3 drops bergamot

'I'm knackered, please make me feel human' aka Exhaustion

- 5 drops peppermint
- 3 drops orange
- 3 drops lemongrass

'Stressed out' aka Stress-Free

- 3 drops frankincense (you are still thinking 'three kings'…)
- 3 drops lavender

When my daughter was seven months old, I started feeling very emotional, tolerance levels were somewhat tested, and my hormones were wild. Experience from my first child told me that this probably wasn't postnatal depression but likely my hormones trying to rebalance post-pregnancy. By chance I spotted that Neal's Yard do an essential oil blend called 'Womens Balance' – I asked the 'stupid' question and was advised this would be perfect to address how I was feeling. Purchase made, and not only do I use it in the diffuser, but I carry it in my bag and will dab it on my wrists if I need a little lift.

Essential oils work for me, they just may work for you.

Effectiveness: 9/10. It amazes me how effective a little bottle of oil can be.

Ease: 8/10. Once you have the kit it is very easy. Effort is required to make the purchase and research the blends.

Budget: Diffusers range from £15–£70. The recommendation is that you purchase decent grade oils, the prices range from £2.50–£15 per oil depending on type/grade. Really worth every penny, and they also make lovely gifts.

TOOL #6
COGNITIVE BEHAVIOURAL THERAPY (CBT)

CBT is simply described as a 'talking therapy', but to me it is so much more. CBT enabled me to release a lot of historical emotional 'baggage' to a completely non-judgemental stranger, who in response encouraged me to challenge the way I think and react to that 'baggage'. During each session I gradually learned more about my own behaviours, the impact they were having on me, and how I could change them to tackle anxiety head-on (i.e. let go).

I am not a medical or mental health professional, so I will point you in the direction of the NHS website to provide a simple overview of what CBT is: www.nhs.uk/conditions/cognitive-behavioural-therapy-cbt/

What CBT did for me:

- Made me realise that I wasn't crazy and I could go a day without the irrational imagination taking over
- Challenged my negative thought processes and eliminated them
- Taught me how to automatically replace negative thinking with positive thoughts
- Showed me that there is no value in looking back; be present, look forward
- Covered childhood experiences that may be the root cause of the anxiety, then not only addressed them but resolved them without the need of anyone else in the room
- Helped me let go of past events that were still influencing my day-to-day life
- Highlighted that I can't change other people's behaviours, but I can change how I react to them and how I can change my own
- Encouraged me to rebuild and release important relationships by questioning/challenging if I wanted/needed those relationships in my life
- Rebuilt my self confidence
- Made me optimistic again
- Turned the fake smiles into real smiles
- Allowed me to LET GO

It was my GP who initially recommended CBT (and then talked about the NHS waiting list); however, I was very fortunate that the company I worked for at the time supported me in funding some of the private sessions. In total I had 15 sessions over a five-month period in 2006/07. I still call upon some of the techniques and Tools I absorbed during what I can honestly describe as some of the most difficult yet ultimately enlightening conversations in my life. All the Tools that I collected during the sessions are covered in this book.

Effectiveness: 10/10 (for me…)

Ease: 6/10. Opening up to a stranger can be very hard and upsetting but the result of doing so can be worth it.

Budget: £40–100 per private session

"You are allowed to change."

(Unknown)

TOOL #7
GRATITUDE VISION BOARD

The Gratitude Vision Board Tool happened by mistake and it was only when we moved house and I hadn't immediately put a new one up that I realised how much it had been lifting me on the down days. Vision boards are powerful positivity Tools. This Gratitude one is so simple yet delivers a regular reminder of all the lovely people and good times in our lives that we are grateful for.

There was a whiteboard on the kitchen wall in a house we rented, so to fill the blank canvas I started to stick up Thank You cards we received, photos of fun times, invites to happy events. Everything up on the board was positive and every time I walked into the kitchen (or did the washing up – admittedly a rare event for me) it was there right in front of me to make me smile and remind me to be thankful for the past, present and future.

So after quickly realising the power the previous board had been having over me, I picked up a new whiteboard in IKEA and popped it up on the new kitchen wall, and it quickly filled with all things positive and all things gratitude. Just the process of doing it made me feel so good, then every day I was receiving both conscious and subconscious happy thoughts when I looked at the board.

What you see is what you feel. What you feel, you focus on. What you focus on becomes reality. I do not think it's a coincidence that when I added dreams and wishes to the board they quickly became a reality.

We have moved again since (I do think this Tool played a part in this unexpected move) and I now have big plans to have a Gratitude & Positivity Vision Wall for the family. I believe it is important to start teaching my children the power of positive thinking and, more importantly, gratitude as early as possible. Now, I haven't quite pulled my finger out on this plan, so in the meantime we have a Gratitude Shelf.

You don't need an actual whiteboard, just a dedicated wall or space in your house that you see daily where you can stick up photos of loved ones, positivity quotes that inspire you, affirmations, Thank You cards, funny memories, postcards from your favourite places or even where you dream of going etc. If you spend a lot of time at a computer screen you could create a Gratitude Screensaver, or if you do a lot of commuting, why not stick some positivity and gratitude to the inside of your sun visor in the car or in the lid of your suitcase?

Try it, you may just be amazed at how great it can make you feel.

Effectiveness: 10/10

Ease: 8/10. Requires some effort to initially put in place; however, the creation process can be really enjoyable.

Budget: Completely up to you. You can pick up whiteboards from as little as £5 online.

TOOL #8
RESCUE REMEDY

At one time, the small yellow bottle filled with five different Bach flowers was a very powerful Tool for me to prevent or quickly reduce the effects of an anxiety attack and quickly restore some inner calm. Whilst most of my friends made sure they had money, their phone and lip gloss when filling their handbag for a night out, for about four years I made sure I had my bottle of Rescue Remedy Spray. Every time.

Rescue Remedy is a natural over-the-counter remedy that can help you get through stressful situations. I have used it in a number of situations, both proactively and reactively, from job interviews and busy days in the office, to girls' nights out and flights. A quick spray and within minutes I would start to feel much calmer. Sometimes just knowing that it was readily available to me could make me feel more at ease.

Simply follow the instructions on the packaging. There are alternatives to the spray, such as drops and pastilles. I have tried most of them; the spray just happens to be the one that worked best for me. It comes in a small bottle, so another useful Tool to have in the back pocket when Tool #1 – Water is not available to you, for example, in airport security.

Rescue Remedy products are also available for children and even pets. If you or a loved one do struggle with stress or anxiety I would definitely recommend that you explore these products.

Effectiveness: 9/10

Ease: 10/10. The spray very easily fits into your back pocket or handbag.

Budget: £5–£10 (depending on product and size) – available from pharmacies, health food stores and supermarkets.

TOOL #9
DAILY SELF-CARE

One of the most important things I have done in the past 12 years for my physical self, mind, emotions and, most importantly, my relationships, is to daily self-care, to have 'ME time' daily. This became even more paramount when I had children. How can I look after tiny humans if I am not looking after myself? How can I teach them to feel good if I'm not feeling good myself? How can I teach them to self-care if I don't set them the example? How can I nag my husband/sister/mother/friends/you (delete as appropriate) to self-care if I don't do it myself? Some call it selfish. I call it essential.

Although self-care can be a visit to a spa for a massage, a hair or nail appointment, a girls' weekend away, an early night when you can grab the opportunity, a spontaneous run or visit to the gym, choosing to eat healthily on a

Monday when you've over-indulged at the weekend, or simply saying 'no' to something you really don't want to do, it really should be so much more. Self-care should be part of your daily routine, no matter how big or small. Everyone deserves a little daily ME time.

Easier said than done?! I used to think so. Then I took a step back, looked at my routine and not only started to introduce new tiny ME times but started to appreciate the ME time that already existed. Now I recognise it as ME time I appreciate it so much more and I am grateful for it, and that in itself is self-care.

Daily self-care will look different to you depending on your lifestyle. It will also change as your life changes. The examples below may not relate to you as these are based on my life today, currently run by two very lovely yet naturally demanding tiny humans aged four years and 17 months, but will give you an idea of how simple ME time can be:

- A five-minute hot shower at the same time every morning to start my day. Just me in the shower cubicle thinking about the day ahead and putting things in order. (Granted, a small child may be banging on the shower door, hence why I also have toys on my bathroom floor at all times to distract them.) I don't start the day without one. Wakes ME.
- On the short car journey after the nursery/school run I consciously change the music on the radio to something uplifting and sing – especially useful if feeling a bit grumpy after a night of wake-ups. Motivates ME.

- The essential oil diffuser is switched on daily – it only takes a few minutes to blend some oils to suit the household's mood. Lifts ME.
- Book ME time in the diary at least once a week as if it is a social event, even if it is for 15 minutes. We book 'no-plan family weekends' in advance to make sure we have 'free family time' at least once a month, so I also book ME time. This is normally on a Saturday morning when I know I can dry my hair without an audience. Builds ME.
- Healthy day at least one day per week. I look at the week ahead and pencil it in the diary. Boosts ME.
- Cook dinner. If it has been a hectic day (and it hasn't been so extreme that it's resulted in a takeaway) and I've successfully achieved the bedtime routine, I really enjoy standing alone in the kitchen creating something for dinner. Just me, a chopping board and the ingredients for a Thai curry can be very therapeutic. Unwinds ME.
- Bath and/or write at least one evening per week (I try and book it in the diary). Relaxes ME.
- Switch the phone off or hide it away for at least 30 minutes every other day. Switches ME off. (Admittedly I am still working on this…)
- No matter the day that has gone before, each night before I go to sleep I say thank you for three positive things that have happened that day. Even if it is as simple as 'Thank you for the hot shower I had this morning'. Don't knock it until you've tried it.

Look after YOU. EVERY DAY. It is important.

Effectiveness: 10/10. Self-care is one of the most effective things you can do for yourself to make yourself feel better.

Ease: 9/10. When you have given yourself some thought this will be easier than you think.

Budget: Completely up to you.

"The relationship with yourself sets the tone for every other relationship you have."

(Jane Travis)

TOOL #10
ACCEPTANCE

This one takes up a whole lot of space in My Wellness Toolbox and I could probably write a whole book about it, but for now I've got one side of A4. Acceptance has to be the most life-changing Tool I have grabbed hold of and sits very nicely alongside Tool #9 – Daily Self-Care. It was during the development of Tool #6 – Cognitive Behavioural Therapy that I was introduced to acceptance, in many ways.

Acceptance can have such a positive impact on your wellbeing, your self-confidence and your relationships. It can also change the way you respond to any negativity that crosses your path; this year it has helped both me and my partner deal with grief.

This is a Tool that you have to work hard at and,

depending on your circumstances, you may choose to seek some professional help to guide you on this one. This Tool not only challenges your existing thought processes but also how you view yourself.

So, what have I accepted in the past 12 years?

- Who I am.
- My flaws. They balance with my strengths.
- My weirdness. That makes me unique.
- My inability to shut up at times. That enables me to meet new people.
- My emotions that hang from my sleeve. They make me human and compassionate.
- My insecurities. They tell my story and I can choose to address them so they don't impact my future story.
- My big round nose with a little bum at the end, which I share with some of the most important people in my life.
- All the good things that I am. Loyal, kind, warm, generous, friendly, funny… and, according to my four-year-old, a very lovely dinosaur.
- That I can't change the past. Live in the present.
- It's happened, it can't be changed. I can either accept it or spend the rest of my life replaying it over and over, punishing myself and others, letting history repeat itself, hurting myself and my relationships. Accept that it happened. Accept that it can't be changed. Accept that it is in my control to let go.
- That what is out of my control is just that. Out of my control.

- Fighting against things that are out of my control will only cause more anxiety and pain for myself and possibly others.
- Uncertainty exists in every situation. Fighting against it will not change that and is only unhelpful to myself.
- That I can't control other people's behaviours, yet I can control my own, which in turn...

For years I placed expectations on a very important person in my life, expectations I didn't share with them; I didn't think I should have to. Surely, they should have known what was expected of them, isn't it textbook? Year on year the resentment grew as those (at times unrealistic) expectations were not met. During a CBT session I was asked why I held on to this relationship that obviously did not make me feel good, more importantly I was challenged on how my behaviours and expectations could be influencing the relationship. I had a few light bulb moments. That evening I phoned the person in question, I swallowed a Thames full of pride and shared with them that I wanted us to have a more positive relationship with more regular contact. That was just over 11 years ago. I accepted the reality, changed my behaviour and today we have a lovely relationship. It is far from textbook – yet so are we. There is nothing wrong with that.

It can be unbelievably hard to accept when something horrendous happens, especially when so many strong emotions have taken over. Therefore, acceptance may not happen overnight: that's OK! Acceptance is not stopping the emotions, ignoring the hurt, rolling over or giving in, it is a way for you to move forward more positively.

Learning to accept has changed my life for the better and also saved the most important relationships in my life.

Effectiveness: 10/10. The hard work seriously pays off. Acceptance can be life-changing.

Ease: 5/10. This requires a lot of mental effort. I had to accept a lot about myself and the role I played in relationships to reap the benefits. Totally worth it.

Budget: Another freebie

"Serenity comes when you trade expectations with acceptance."

(Buddha)

TOOL #11
AFFIRMATIONS

Affirmations are positive quotes/statements/phrases that you can repeat to yourself out loud or in your head, reminding or telling yourself how you want to feel, what you want to be and even what you want to achieve. You can also write your favourite ones down, put them in your purse, hang them on your wall, stick them on your desk at work and include them on your vision boards – just make them very present in your life.

I have used affirmations for many years to override negative thinking with positive thoughts. When I was at my most anxious, my mind was riddled with negative thinking that at times scared me and eventually chipped away at my self-confidence; it was a vicious circle. I then learned to start interrupting those negative thoughts with positive affirmations. It didn't take too long before I realised something had changed. Positivity was no longer the exception, it was the rule. More importantly, my confidence had started to return.

Affirmations are a powerful Tool to use when in the midst of facing fears or feeling anxious. I used to be terrified of hospitals, the thought of even walking in the main entrance would make me dizzy, but when I fell pregnant I had the realisation I was just going to have to get over it, for not only me but my baby (one of the main drivers for doing hypnobirthing – a Tool coming soon), so I introduced some affirmations specifically to address those fears. They worked!

When you begin using affirmations you may not really believe the affirmation is true, but the more you repeat it, again and again, you will come to truly believe it and in turn that affirmation will become reality.

Here are some examples:

- I love and trust myself.
- I am a loving, thoughtful and caring person surrounded by positivity.
- I am open to the lessons that today brings me.
- I accept what I cannot change and move on.
- I am surrounded by people who care and support me in everything I do.
- I have a healthy body, a healthy mind and a healthy soul.
- I can handle today in a positive and calm way.
- I am a good and honest friend and attract positive friendships.

- I am a wonderful mummy and make my children happy.
- I believe in myself.
- I am rich in all areas of my life.
- I am unique and that is one of my biggest strengths.
- I have courage to face what is ahead of me today.
- I attract good fortune.
- I sleep peacefully knowing a fresh day awaits me.
- I will achieve my goal.
- I can lose this weight easily. (Think it's time I started using this one…)

One of my all-time favourites:

- I am enough.

Affirmations are for everyone! Give them a go and just watch what happens…

Effectiveness: 9/10. The more you use affirmations the more effective they become.

Ease: 8/10. Requires some thought but when you've got the hang of it they flow to you very easily.

Budget: FREE!!!

TOOL #12
NO

How many of you want to say 'no' to something but find yourself saying 'yes' because it feels like the right or the easiest thing to do for someone else, even if it is not the right or easiest thing for you. If this resonates with you then grab this Tool, put it in your box and, most importantly, use it.

I was (and admittedly still am at times) a people pleaser. Especially in my earlier IT Service career, it was the norm for me to say 'yes' to doing things outside of my role, taking on extra work, going above and beyond the call of duty, working extra hours, not for my own gain but to please my customers, my management or my co-workers. It was pretty much guaranteed that if you asked me to do something I would say 'yes', so it became expected. I also hated the thought of letting anyone down. 'Yes' was the easier option all round, wasn't it?!

My ego may have taken a rub, I'm sure my eagerness to get involved and to go the extra mile was a good quality to further my career, but with everything else going on in life that I was also saying 'yes' to, my soul was being worn down… and eventually wore out. This wasn't good for anyone.

When I took a step back and looked at where I could make life easier for myself, I realised quite quickly I had to start saying 'no' to things I really didn't want to do. I had to learn to be more assertive. Growing up, my mum would always say to me, "Please do whatever you want in this life – as long as it doesn't hurt yourself or another, then go for it." I decided to apply this advice to when I said 'no' and it's only writing this down now that I realise another affirmation is born: "I can say 'no'. As long as it doesn't intentionally hurt me or another, I can say 'no' when I want or need to with confidence".

Not long after I started to use this Tool with some force, I was in a 1-2-1 with a senior member of the team at work. They had played a very supportive role when I had hit rock bottom and wanted to let me know how pleased they were to see me "getting back on track", and with tongue in cheek they said "… it's just not so great for me as you have become so good at using the word no". Many a true word spoken in jest.

When I started using the word 'no', it sometimes felt scary as I prepared to say it, then a rush of relief came once it had fallen off the tongue and then a massive sense of empowerment when done.

If the thought of using this Tool brings you out in a cold sweat, take it slowly. Start saying 'no' to small things and build up to the big stuff over time. Try to avoid using elaborate excuses to justify your 'no'. Keep it simple, be straightforward and honest, and more importantly be respectful. It may feel uncomfortable to begin with but the more you use this Tool, the easier it becomes.

Not only did this Tool give me some breathing space and time, I found that some people even started to respect me more as I set new expectations and boundaries. However, it also confused some around me and some friendships changed. This is the downside to this Tool; you may find people who are used to you being a 'yes' people pleaser do not like the new 'no' in you. I have been called stubborn, selfish, awkward, even competitive, and no doubt much more behind my back, when all I have done is said 'no' to things that they would normally expect me to say 'yes' to.

Fortunately, the downside is nothing compared to the positive impact it will have on YOU. In the long term, YOU will feel less resentment and so much more confident for making the right choices for YOU to do what YOU want in life. You will also become very aware of the people in your life who respect your wellbeing: they are the keepers.

Always think of this Tool when you are asking someone to do something for you. If they are hesitant, be supportive. Do not put pressure on people to say 'yes' for your gain as you don't know what negative impact this could have on them.

Of course, this is real life – there will be some

circumstances where 'no' may not be an option. This is also your life, respect yourself – if 'no' is an option, then use it.

Effectiveness: 7/10. When you get the hang of this Tool and it becomes the norm for you it can be very effective. However, be prepared that some people will challenge you along the way, which may make you feel uncomfortable – so pair this Tool with Tool #2 – Breathe.

Ease: 6/10. This is out the comfort zone and requires a large dollop of confidence if it is not the norm for you. It is worth it though!

Budget: Nothing for a 'no'.

"It's only by saying 'no' that you can concentrate on the things that are really important."

(Steve Jobs)

TOOL #13
SELF-HELP BOOKS

In 2005, in the depth of anxiety, I was desperate for an answer and so I purchased what would be my first very own self-help book, *Change Your Life in 7 Days* by Paul McKenna. This would become a very important Tool to help me change my life.

Now this book didn't quite change my life in seven days, but by the end of the week it had encouraged me to start changing the way I was looking at my life. It gave me a new perspective, started to educate me on the power of positivity, made me really consider what my dreams were and gave me some powerful anchor Tools that I still use today.

During a house move in 2011 this book would find itself packed away in a box marked 'books to keep'. The box remained unopened and has moved to a new house four times again since. I may not be reading the books everyday, but I still use the Tools they provided me with on a regular basis. These books are keepers.

So today, for research purposes, the box was opened, and I took a look inside. I flicked through *Change Your Life in 7 Days* and was gobsmacked when I turned to page 142 and as part of the dream-setting exercise written down were eight goals I had set myself 13 years ago... and seven out of eight have been achieved! I had a little cry (happy tears) and have decided to share the goals with you to show that if you are open to using self-help books, they can give you Tools that really work.

When I wrote these goals down in 2005, they were dreams that at the time the anxiety deemed completely impossible, but with the Tools in My Wellness Toolbox, anxiety was proved wrong and they became a reality. The dates are when I achieved the goals.

✓ Reduce and remove anxiety – 2007
✓ Laugh EVERY DAY – 2007
✓ Change role within two years – in 2006 I got the promotion I wanted that led to some great opportunities and ultimately my first business
✓ Spend more time with Dad – in 2006 we both agreed to put more effort in and now have a positive relationship with regular contact
✓ Go on safari – 2010
✓ Marry Matt – 2013... it turned out to be a different Matt that I married – but hey, I still married Matt!!

✓ Ask Ali Ltd – in 2011 we started trading and we are still going strong

I am yet to publish a poem… there is still time…

A few years later in 2009, following a difficult and upsetting period, which took me several steps backwards, I came across another Paul McKenna book called *Control Stress – Stop Worrying and Feel Good Now*.

This book introduced to me to the Calm Anchor, which is an associative conditioning Tool. In simple terms, the Calm Anchor exercises from the book enabled me to train my brain to respond in a certain way when I performed a specific action. Now, when in stressful situations, if I press my thumb and middle finger together my head is flooded with positive thoughts about myself, which can make me instantly calmer. It is so effective for me that in more recent years there have been occasions where I have been in an everyday situation that in the past I deemed very stressful (for example, shopping in a supermarket) and my head will suddenly flood with all things positive, and I'll then realise my thumb and middle finger are glued together! Safe to say, my subconscious has hard-wired this Tool.

In the book, McKenna describes that 'In the same way as the anchor of a boat helps keep it steady in the midst of stormy seas, an emotional anchor helps you to stay calm in the midst of your daily life, but unlike the anchor of a boat, an emotional anchor becomes stronger the more you use it'. Very true.

Over the years I have bought several self-help books,

normally based on recommendation, to help me address something and/or for research and study purposes. Some worked for me, some didn't, what works for me may not work for you and vice versa. The most useful books for me are the ones that contain exercises as they help me stay focused.

In addition to the above, if you experience anxiety, have fears you struggle to face or are struggling to let go of something, then I would also recommend:

✓ *Feel the Fear & Do It Anyway* – Susan Jeffers
✓ *Feel the Fear ... and Beyond* – Susan Jeffers
✓ *You Can Heal Your Life* – Louise Hay

Effectiveness: 9/10. They work for me! You may go through a few books to find the right one for you, but when you do that book will remain on the shelf or in the 'books to keep' box forever!

Ease: 7/10. This one requires some effort to research and purchase the right book for you, then normally you have to do some work. This can be enjoyable for some but an effort for others. It does pay off!

Budget: Average £10 for a paperback but some books can be as little as £0.99 for the Kindle edition.

TOOL #14
POSITIVE PEOPLE

Every choice we make is influenced by the people in our lives. So, when choosing the Tools for your Wellness Toolbox I would highly recommend you grasp Tool #14 – Positive People with both hands and make it essential.

When you surround yourself with positive people it not only makes you happier and can improve your health and wellbeing, but it also makes you far more aware of those who are not a positive influence in your life. You can then make the choice to stand back from those who don't enrich and support you and spend time with those who want to help you grow.

Think about what a positive person looks like for you.

For me, positive people focus on the good things in their life and are friendly, warm, easy to talk with, trustworthy, supportive of the decisions I make, able to share and celebrate both our successes, honest with me, compassionate, encouraging, energetic and fun to be with. They bring out the best in me.

And someone who is not a positive person?

A person that is not a positive influence in my life focuses on the negative, may make me feel anxious in their company, makes me feel drained after spending time with them, criticises my character, judges me and talks negatively about me and others, displays jealousy and does not support or celebrate my growth.

Can you easily identify the positive people in your life?

Those who are not positive for you are not always bad or toxic people (although sadly some of these do exist), they may not even realise the negative influence they can have on you, but if someone does not make you feel good then either tell them so you can attempt to make changes together and improve your relationship, or take a step back and spend less time with them. If this is not possible, make the choice that you will not allow their negative ways to influence your emotions, behaviours and choices.

It can be a challenge to take a step back from family and friends as these can be deep-rooted, complex relationships. It can be even more difficult to distance yourself from work colleagues who you may have to sit next to for eight hours a day, but you can choose how you let them affect you.

You do not have to fall out with someone to take a step back, you can choose to spend less time with them and more time with the positive people and activities in your life. Also, it does not have to be forever; some breathing space and having time out from someone can strengthen a relationship and remind you of all the positive things you do bring to each other's lives.

However, if there is someone in your life whose behaviour or attitude is continually having a negative impact on your health and wellbeing then think about Tools #9 – Self-Care and #10 – Acceptance and try to do something about it, even if the first step is to talk to someone about how you are feeling.

It was during my most anxious days that the positive people in my life stood out so clearly to me. I chose to spend more time with them, I made plans with them and I felt a lot of gratitude towards them. They are the keepers in my life.

The more time I spent with people that made me feel good the happier I became, I laughed more, I became less anxious and more positive people kept appearing in my life, including the guy who is now my husband.

The importance of this Tool became even clearer to me when I stepped on to the rollercoaster that is parenthood. You need supporters, not competitors, on this journey. It is no coincidence that new friends that we have attracted (and vice versa) have been like-minded, positive influences in our family life.

It may require you to take a deep breath of confidence to strike a conversation with the colleague that smiles at you every day in the corridor, or to message the old friend who you always used to laugh with, but life got in the way, or to ask the friendly mum at the school gate if you can

49

arrange a play date, or to go and sign up for that <insert hobby here> class to meet like-minded people that love the same activities that you do. When you do these things, this is when you will begin to attract positive people to your life.

And most importantly, always remember that positivity is a magnet. Positivity attracts positivity. So always choose to be one of the positive people.

Effectiveness: 10/10. Positive people are one of the most effective Tools in My Wellness Toolbox, they really rub off on you!!

Ease: 6/10. The more positive you are, the easier you will attract positive people. This may require you to make difficult choices to step back from those who may not be positive influences in your life.

Budget: Positive people enrich you, they don't cost a thing!

"I have found my tribe, people who inspire me daily and I inspire them too. I have found a home where my strengths are praised and my challenges are worked on daily, without shame, embarrassment or judgement."

(Holly Miller)

TOOL #15
GRATITUDE

Gratitude is my favourite proactive Tool. Gratitude has helped me maintain positivity through major life-changing events, reminds me of how far I have come on the down days, continually boosts my wellbeing and prevents anxiety.

I like to think I have always been a thankful and appreciative person but it was not until six years ago when I was introduced to some incredible books called *The Secret* and *The Power* (Tool #18 – coming soon) that I started to consciously practise Gratitude daily and very quickly I started to see my life transform to a whole new level; some amazing, at times quite unbelievable, things started to happen.

Gratitude is not just saying 'thank you', it is a happy

emotion that I not only feel when someone does something nice for me, but I feel when I appreciate all that surrounds me, in my past, my present and my future.

To begin with you must focus hard and put in some effort to practice Gratitude, however it does not take long for this Tool to become part of your daily life; now it is just part of who I am. I practice Gratitude in many ways:

Thank You

Every day when I wake up, I say 'thank you' for at least three positive things that will happen that day:

- Thank you for the fantastic news that today will bring.
- Thank you for my children having a happy and safe day at nursery.
- Thank you for the training course that I will be able to focus on easily.

Throughout my day, I aim to remember to be grateful for the things that are easy to take for granted:

- Thank you for the comfy bed that we wake up in every day.
- Thank you for the gorgeous views we see every day on the school run.
- Thank you for the food in the fridge that keeps my family well fed and healthy.

Throughout my day, if I catch myself being irritated by something or someone, I try to find a reason to be grateful:

- Thank you for the traffic jam that has given me a chance to stop for a moment and take a deep breath.

- Thank you for my appointment being cancelled at the last minute as it gave me a chance to have some unexpected ME time.
- Thank you for the shoes I have just fallen over in the hallway as it means my husband has arrived home safely. (Through gritted teeth!)

And every night before I go to sleep, I aim to say 'thank you' for at least three positive things that have happened that day.

Gratitude Diary Entries

I have already written many Gratitude diary entries for the year ahead in my diary. For example, in February we are due to pay the remaining balance for our annual holiday, so I have already written into the future, 'thank you for funds that have come to us easily to pay for our incredible holiday'.

A very important person in my life has a hospital appointment for some significant tests. I have written next to the date the appointment is booked on, 'I am grateful for the NHS care <VIP> is receiving and the good results <VIP> will receive'.

Throughout the year I will continue to write 'thank you' next to random dates and for key events. These will include dates that we look forward to (e.g. weddings, holidays) and, more importantly, dates that may make us feel apprehensive or anxious (e.g. hospital appointments, job interviews). I have been doing this since 2013 and I know it works. The Gratitude diary dates are always memorable for the right reasons. Give it a go and be gobsmacked!!

Gratitude Notebook

At least once a month I will find some time when utilising Tool #9 – Self-Care to sit and write all the things I am grateful for in my Gratitude Notebook. This tends to cover the big stuff:

* I am grateful for all my lovely family and friends and the good times we share.
* I am grateful for the exciting opportunities that SisterGoodness is bringing my sister and me.
* I am grateful for all the NHS teams that have provided my family and me with amazing healthcare, including the safe arrival of my babies.

Gratitude Notes

In my purse I have a $1 banknote with a message saying 'thank you for all the money I have been given throughout my life'. When I open my purse, I see the note and I am constantly reminded to show Gratitude for the good fortune that comes into my life.

Gratitude Texts & Gifts

I send 'out of the blue' texts or gifts to family and friends to let them know that I am grateful for having them in my life and that I am thinking of them. Giving is receiving when it comes to Gratitude.

Gratitude can instantly lift your mood, especially when you are feeling tired or stressed. This will then have a positive knock-on effect for your health, wellbeing and relationships. Just writing about Gratitude has made me feel good. I hope you find this Tool just as powerful and as motivating as I do.

Effectiveness: 10/10. This Tool should not be optional.

Ease: 10/10 to say 'thank you', 7/10 to practice Gratitude every day.

Budget: It costs nothing to be grateful.

TOOL #16
LET GO & RELEASE TECHNIQUES

Letting go is easier said than done. Personally, I find it quite hard to let go purely by thinking about letting go, especially on the other side of an argument, if I am in the midst of feeling anxious, going through a stressful time or staring a fear in the face. Therefore, along my journey, as soon as I come across 'letting go' techniques that make me physically feel like I am letting go of the argument, the anxiety, the stress or the fear, I grab it and in My Wellness Toolbox it goes.

The Pebble Technique
Following a heartbreak when I was still experiencing regular anxiety attacks, I was walking along my favourite

beach in the world (in Pembrokeshire, Wales) and picked up a pebble. I have no idea what led me to start talking to the pebble but before I knew it the poor pebble was not only having to develop listening skills but was having to deal with tears, a lot of tears. Then in a surge of emotion I catapulted the pebble into the sea. Oh, it felt good. I instantly stopped crying and started smiling. I picked up another pebble, spilt a whole load of emotions over it and launched it into the waves. This was working. It felt like an instant release. I felt exhilarated when I left the beach and a sense of assurance; everything was really going to be OK. It was definitely a turning point to me moving forward at that difficult time.

I have used the Pebble Technique to throw all sorts of things into the deep sea, including anxiety and panic attacks. It is a powerful way to release and let things go.

Just in case you won't be visiting the seaside any time soon, pebbles and the sea can be replaced with stones and the canal/river/pond/drain. You get the gist!

Just a few weeks ago I came across something called a 'worry pebble'. I had never seen or heard of these before. They are smooth, polished heart-shaped pebbles. The guidance (according to a Google search) is that when you are feeling stressed or worried you roll the pebble between your fingers and it helps you relax. It made me think that this same little worry pebble could also be used to release your worries too, a very small but useful Tool that can go with you everywhere.

Nature is always happy to help.

The WIDABI (Write It Down And Burn It) Technique

I have worked in IT for the past 20 years – I was always going to throw in an acronym at some point. WIDABI is the one!

WIDABI may be a subconscious reason why I have always wished for a real fire at home, because now that I have got one, this technique is getting more exercise than ever before. It is very straightforward:

You will need…
1) Paper and pen
2) Fire (anything from a lit match to a bonfire)

What you do…
-   On a piece of paper write down what you want to let go of. This may be a fear, a worry, a situation, a memory, a person, anything. (We refer to it as 'It'.)
-   You can write down one word or a novel – up to you
-   Be grateful for any lessons that you have learned from It
-   Say 'goodbye' to any negativity It created
-   Release It into the fire
-   Let It go
-   Watch It physically burn away
-   Feel the benefits within minutes/hours/days

I shared WIDABI with a lady who I felt was a little sceptical that this technique could help her release a specific frustration she has had with her partner for quite a few years, related to her partner's inability to clean up properly after they cook dinner (I do not think she is alone). She was prepared to give it a go.

She wrote down her frustration, then as she started to talk about the lessons learned from It she had a realisation moment. She probably spends more words complaining about the untidy kitchen than she does saying 'thank you' for her partner cooking dinner. The reason for letting It go had more than one motivation. She said 'goodbye' (to her negativity) and released It into the fire.

A few days later she fed back that it had worked. That re-occurring frustration had gone. Maybe this was the result of the WIDABI Technique working alongside the new feelings of gratitude.

Fear Release Technique

I was introduced to the Fear Release Technique when I was pregnant and attending hypnobirthing classes (… another Tool coming soon) but you do not need to be pregnant to use this technique as it can be applied to any situation that may be creating anxiety or worries for you.

As an apprehensive new mummy- (and daddy-) to-be, we were asked to write down any anxieties, worries, concerns, doubts, fears etc that we had about having our baby (obviously you could apply this to any situation). This was interesting as things came to the surface that I/we hadn't consciously worried about until that moment; this was giving us an opportunity to release them immediately before they jumped out unexpectedly. We then talked about the fears with each other and replaced each one with a positive affirmation.

For example, I was really worried about feeling anxious during labour and passing the anxiety to my baby. Therefore, I wrote the fear down, discussed the fear to help 'neutralise' it and then replaced it with the positive affirmation 'I will be calm and focused during the birth of my baby'. I then used the affirmation through the last few months of my pregnancy.

32 hours into labour I ended up in an ambulance, blue lights flashing with an emergency C-section to follow, everyone around me could not believe how calm and focused I remained during a situation that would make anyone extremely anxious and scared. This stuff really works.

I have since used the Fear Release Technique for Baby No. 2 and job interviews.

So is it time you let It go? Try one or all of these techniques and watch It be replaced with a dose of relief and happiness.

Effectiveness: 9/10. All these techniques work for me, although for the really deep-rooted stuff it may require a few applications!!

Ease: 9/10. For me this is one of the easiest Tools to use in My Wellness Toolbox – just don't overthink it!

Budget: It depends how close you live to the beach or how big your fire needs to be! But seriously, this Tool costs very little or nothing at all.

"What if letting go isn't the end but the beginning of your happiness?"

(Unknown)

TOOL #17
REIKI

Reiki was introduced to me during a pregnancy massage when I was pregnant with my first child. It not only put me in a much-needed deep state of relaxation during the treatment, but it relieved my physical hip and back pain, which at times was getting me down. Most importantly for the few days following, it gave me sleep; lovely deep, uninterrupted sleep. A few months after the birth it would also become an invaluable Tool to chill me out and help me deal with some of the anxieties and worries that new motherhood brings. One hour with Jaki and I would walk out recharged and ready for the next dirty nappy.

I could not fathom how on Earth the lovely Jaki was exactly doing what she was doing by simply placing her hot hands on me or within my aura, but whatever it was that she was doing, this complementary therapy worked, and I went back for more… and more. Reiki is possibly one of the most-used Tools in My Wellness Toolbox.

I was so impressed by the results on my health and wellbeing that in 2016, when pregnant with my second child, I decided to learn more about Reiki and booked myself on a Reiki Level 1 training course. I finally 'got it' and after I experienced a much calmer self and witnessed the benefits it had on settling my windy baby and my, at times distraught "because I wanted to get the cereal out the cupboard not you", threenager, I knew I wanted to continue my Reiki journey further and became Reiki Level 2 attuned in November 2017. In March 2018 I qualified as a Reiki Practitioner.

So, what is Reiki? The following description is taken from www.reiki.org/faq/whatisreiki.html:

Reiki is a Japanese technique for stress reduction and relaxation that also promotes healing. It is administered by "laying on hands" and is based on the idea that an unseen "life force energy" flows through us and is what causes us to be alive. If one's "life force energy" is low, then we are more likely to get sick or feel stress, and if it is high, we are more capable of being happy and healthy.

A treatment feels like a wonderful glowing radiance that flows through and around you. Reiki treats the whole person including body, emotions, mind and spirit, creating many beneficial effects that include relaxation and feelings of peace, security and wellbeing. Many have reported miraculous results.

Reiki is a simple, natural and safe method of spiritual healing and self-improvement that everyone can use. It has been effective in helping virtually every known illness and malady and always creates a beneficial effect. It also works in conjunction with all other medical or therapeutic techniques to relieve side effects and promote recovery.

I have been challenged several times on my belief in Reiki. I can understand why people are sceptical; I had doubts and these led me to educate myself. I also do not expect everyone to have the same belief system as me. I just feel very fortunate that Reiki is something that came into my life and it is something I am now very passionate about. It has brought me, my children, my husband, my family and my friends so much benefit.

As part of working towards becoming a Reiki Level 2 practitioner I was required to work with a number of case studies and give over 75 hours of Reiki. These are just some of the benefits Reiki has given to those I have worked with:

- Physical pain reduced
- Sleep improved
- Anxiety reduced
- Stress reduced
- Confidence levels increased
- Tolerance levels increased (aka the ability to "not give

a 5h1t" as much increased)
- Ability to relax improved
- Clarity
- Life-changing decision made!!!!! Eeeeek!
- In the word of one case study, "Zen"

There have been a few jaw-dropping moments. One of the case studies advised that since session two (of four) they had not used any painkillers for their rheumatoid and osteopathic arthritis (they typically can take up to eight painkillers in 24 hours). Even though I know Reiki works, I had not appreciated it could work so fast. Then, following session four, the same case study had an appointment with their consultant to review the condition of their hip. The expectation had been set six months previously that the hip would need to be replaced this year. The consultant appeared confused when looking at the latest x-ray, he asked what had changed as the hip had showed vast improvement and a replacement was no longer required at this time, and he set a new expectation of five years. The case study advises that the only thing that has changed is that she is now having Reiki!

You can find Reiki therapists all over the country. Personal recommendations are normally best. If you do know someone locally who has Reiki and they are happy with their therapist, why not give this complementary therapy a try?

Effectiveness: 10/10. Reiki has been very effective for me for both physical and mental needs.

Ease: 10/10. You just need to lie back and let someone else work with the energy.

Budget: Approx. £30–£60 per hour depending on location and experience of therapist

Five Reiki Principles

Do Not Be Angry
Do Not Worry
Be Grateful
Work with Diligence
Be Kind to People

(Mikao Usui)

TOOL #18
THE SECRET, THE POWER, THE MAGIC

In 2011 we set up our own IT Consultancy business and I found myself working away from home five days a week in Staines. This is where I would meet a lovely lady from Liverpool called Angela. This is where Angela would introduce me to a book called *The Secret* (by Rhonda Byrne). This book would soon become a significant and uplifting Tool in My Wellness Toolbox... the sequels, called *The Power* and *The Magic*, soon followed.

Angela and I were sharing stories over a meal after work one evening as we got to know each other. She asked me how I had found myself in Staines doing what I was doing. I started to talk about my dreams of working hard in IT to enable us to save enough money to buy a house, that at some point we would want to get married and maybe have a family, we planned to travel more, I would prefer to be working closer to home, that I had a wish to write a book to help others who had experienced anxiety, at some point I would like to become a career/life/wellness coach. I talked about my concerns of anxiety returning, that although I knew I had come a long way I still lacked self-belief. Angela then asked with a grin: "If these are your dreams why are you not doing them now?" I looked confused and replied, "Err… because I can't do it all at the same time." She smiled and said, "If you say so. Do one thing tonight when you get back to your room – order a copy of a book called *The Secret* by Rhonda Byrne. I'm not going to explain why, just do it." Intrigued, I did just that.

The Secret arrived a few days later. I actually struggled to get into it to begin with, but I persevered, and it was this book that helped me really understand the Law of Attraction – that what I think about is what I will attract; positive thoughts attract positive outcomes. Throughout, Rhonda highlights the importance of using visualisation and gratitude to achieve and obtain all the things you want in life. I had been introduced to these concepts from other self-help books, but this took me to a whole new level.

One of the first exercises in the book is very simple but very quickly highlights the way Law of Attraction works. It encourages you to focus on parking your car in a car park with ease. As it happened at that time, every Monday morning I struggled to park on the clients' site, it was the day I had a long commute and by the time I arrived at

8.30am there were never any spaces left. I used to worry and flare my nostrils about it every week. So, I grasped this exercise with both hands.

I visualised me parking with ease. I imagined the area of the car park I would go to, that there in front of me would be the empty space. I was grateful that the car park had a space for me. I trusted and believed this would work.

It did. Every single week.

I never had a problem parking again. It became a joke in the office; it was my Monday morning challenge, my colleagues asked me what I was offering security to save me a space. I wasn't offering them anything. It seems crazy. I understand why some of you may be rolling your eyes as you read this, but it worked. It carried on working. It carried on working because I changed my way of thinking, retuned and enhanced my belief system. I have applied this to so many areas of my life, with jaw-dropping results.

The more I used *The Secret* the more my self-belief and confidence grew. I finally believed that my own thoughts can create and impact outcomes. I realised why Angela directed me to this book. She recognised that although I had overcome the anxiety, I had not let go of it completely; now was the time to truly believe in myself and my mind, to let go of the negativity and outdated belief system that was holding me back, to be grateful and focus on turning those dreams into reality.

The Power is next in the series. This really helped me put everything I learned in *The Secret* into practice. It guides you to focus on giving love and gratitude to bring positivity into your life. Again, some of it I can't explain, but when you start putting the theory into practice, amazing things really do start to happen.

The Magic, book number three, has 28 daily gratitude exercises to bring you happiness and abundance. You start on Day 1 by 'Counting your Blessings', by Day 8 it is 'The Magic Ingredient', being thankful for the food you eat. Day 19 is 'Magic Footsteps', 100 steps of thanks. My personal favourite is Day 27, 'The Magic Mirror' – do not forget to thank yourself. This book enabled me to really understand and start using Tool #15 – Gratitude effectively.

The author, Rhonda Byrne, has faced a lot of criticism about these books. I am not here to challenge those critics and I do not intend to; all I know is that I read these books, I put the theories into practice and many incredible things have happened in my life since. I will continue to take from these books what I believe.

You will find *The Secret*, *The Power* and *The Magic* on the same shelf as Tool #13 – Self-Help Books. Due to the positive impact this series of books has had on my life perspective and the many ways they have taught me how to use Tool #15 – Gratitude, they must stand out as their very own Tool. The teachings from these books are with me 24/7, although admittedly I (and my husband) often need to give myself a nudge to remind me to use them, especially on the sleep-deprived days.

I have given so many copies of *The Secret* away to friends over the last few years and I have seen this Tool work for them in so many positive ways for their health, emotions, wellbeing and fortune. This Tool may just be worth a try for you.

Effectiveness: 10/10. For me these books were a game changer and the teachings are now with me 24/7.

Ease: 7/10. I struggled to get into *The Secret* to begin with, but I persevered, kept practising and reaped the rewards. I found *The Power* and *The Magic* a lot easier to absorb and put into practice. *The Secret* is also a film and is available on DVD.

Budget: Prices range from £7.50–£12 per book (hardback/paperback/Kindle edition). *The Secret* DVD is approx. £14. All available on Amazon.

"Never let a day pass without looking for the good, feeling the good within you, praising, appreciating, blessing, and being grateful. Make it your life commitment, and you will stand in utter awe of what happens in your life."

(Rhonda Byrne)

TOOL #19

MASSAGE THERAPIES

Warning: this Tool is addictive.

The nineteenth Tool in My Wellness Toolbox is not just about taking the time out to relax to soothe your aches and pains. Massage therapies can bring a wealth of benefits to your physical and mental wellbeing. Proven to boost immunity, soothe anxiety and depression, reduce the overwhelming feeling of stress, improve your sleep, improve your mood, make you feel more energised… and so much more.

Over the years I have been very lucky to have experienced all kinds of massages. These are my top five:

Lava Shell Massage

Love. Love. Love. Similar to a hot stone massage but in my opinion much more effective. I feel super relaxed yet energised after an hour of having hot, smooth tiger clam shells massaged into all areas of my body with varying techniques and pressure. Not only does this type of massage enable deep tissue work, removing knots in my neck and easing muscle tension all over, but the heat gets the blood supply pumping so it can aid in eliminating all those toxic waste products – better out than in. I often fall asleep during a lava shell massage, have been known to cry following a treatment – a good thing to release those blocked up emotions – and always feel uplifted as I reluctantly leave the massage table.

Indian Head Massage

If you struggle to switch off during a massage therapy, or you need to empty your head of negative self-talk and unwanted thoughts, then a good Indian head massage may be for you. I call it 'empty head massage', as following a treatment I literally struggle to think about anything.

This relaxing massage works specifically on the shoulders, upper back, head, scalp, neck and face. It is also beneficial for relieving headaches and migraines and, as it encourages the supply of oxygen to your brain, it is also a great mood booster... and apparently a good Indian head massage also promotes hair growth!!

Just be prepared to wash your hair afterwards,

especially if the therapist uses lovely warm oils as part of the treatment. Divine.

Reflexology

If you do not like your feet being touched, then this is NOT the treatment for you. I, however, love the sensation of reflexology and within minutes of the treatment starting I drop into a very deep state of relaxation. This is very good for bringing me back down to earth during stressful periods.

Reflexology is a complementary and holistic therapy with the aim of restoring balance to your body naturally and comes with a heap of benefits. I personally use it for relaxation as I know it will zone me out so quickly. I also find it helps when the digestion system needs some encouragement. I am normally more energised at the end of a session so it is especially useful when feeling tired and lethargic.

Technically, reflexology is not a massage. On the soles, tops and sides of the feet there are reflexes which correspond to different areas of the body. Your reflexologist will use specialised massage techniques, using their thumbs, fingers and knuckles, to apply pressure to specific reflex points on your feet. More pressure will be applied if the reflexologist picks up on potential pain, tightness or congestion that needs to be relieved. Some of the benefits can be realised during the treatment, such as relaxation; however, you may notice others, such as pain relief, up to 24–48 hours later. It is clever stuff and yet another opportunity to put your feet up for an hour and self-care.

Aromatherapy Massage

I love an Aromatherapy Massage, especially as it makes great use of Tool #5 – Essential Oils, and brings me multiple benefits during the treatment. I consider them to be quite indulgent so tend to have them as a treat on holiday or around my birthday.

As I lie there sinking into the massage, I gradually switch off as I inhale the lovely smells from the oils that are also penetrating my skin, so working on the inside too. I also find they soothe my eczema that often flares during stressful periods or if I am feeling burnt out.

A good therapist will give you a choice of oil blends to pick from. I always seek advice from the therapist, so we can match them to my mood; this means I get the most benefit from the treatment. I always walk away feeling relaxed or energised. Mood boosted? Tick.

Naked Massage

As I am sure you have now gathered, I love a good massage. So, when travelling in Asia I took full advantage of the low prices. During our group tour in India I booked in for my first travelling massage, arranged by our "I have a friend who can do this" tour guide (he had a lot of friends). I decided to go all in and agreed to a full body massage. My husband who at the time was not a 'massage goer' (and still isn't – but that is another hilarious story), decided he would embrace the travelling experiences and booked in for a hand massage as he was a bit worried about what a full body massage may entail; he did not want to feel

78

exposed. This created much amusement amongst the travelling group, so after much assurance (and bullying) from a few of us, at the last minute he opted for a full body massage too…

Now, I am used to a Western and 'conservative' approach to massage. The private room, the comfy bed, the towels and sheets to cover your modesty, the therapist who leaves the room to give you time to undress and prepare yourself on the table… my expectations were very naïve, even narrow-minded. That was short-lived.

Imagine walking into a spacious room. In front of you are two large solid wooden blocks with steps – you quickly realise these are the massage tables for you and another who you met a few days before. No curtains. No towels. No sheets. A therapist who watches you intently throughout as you undress, and she says only one word – "naked"! WHAT!!!! She hands you what can only be described as a cotton wire to cover your modesty and directs you with her hands to lie on your back on the wooden block. That's it. You. Lying there. Naked.

The massage begins, it's ticklish and, despite every attempt not to, the child in you starts giggling. Then the realisation your husband is having the same experience hits you. You feel bad for a few seconds. Then start giggling again. Another also starts giggling. The therapists, who do not know why we are giggling, also start giggling, nervously. Awkward yet hilarious.

I struggled to even think about relaxing but the actual massage, although a bit too thorough at times, was very good. It became even more awkward at the end of the massage when I was ushered to sit up as the therapist then washed me down with a cloth. The cotton wire had dissolved. Exposed.

I will never forget the face of my husband as he walked out of his treatment room. Oh, how we laughed. We opted against another naked massage on our travels, but this massage experience brought us so much laughter, the greatest Tool of all, it had to make the top five.

Investing in a good massage is investing in yourself. Do it.

Effectiveness: 9/10. It is very rare that a massage therapy doesn't relax and/or recharge me.

Ease: 9/10. Feet up and enjoy. The hardest part is finding a therapist that you connect with, but the journey to find one is still very enjoyable.

Budget: This really does depend on location, type and length of treatment and experience of therapist. In my experience, UK and Europe prices vary from £30–£100 per hour. Head to Asia and you can pay as little as £2 for a Thai foot massage.

TOOL #20
LEARN SOMETHING NEW

In 2006, just a few months before I hit my rock bottom, I qualified as a rugby union referee. That was during my darkest year, yet those three hours I would spend in the RFU classroom each week were a positive light that I would look forward to. In those three hours I could redirect my overthinking negative brain to learn something new. Learning is escapism; not only can it help you break normal patterns of behaviour by taking the time to do something different, it can be enjoyable and rewarding at the same time. When I passed the exam with flying colours I felt a huge sense of achievement and it reminded me that I was good at something, giving my self-confidence a much-needed tickle.

Disappointingly, my confidence was not ready to take

the new acquired skills on to the actual rugby pitch; the thought would make me feel physically sick and therefore I kept avoiding the opportunity. I have to admit that I never put all that hard work and training into practice with 30 fit rugby players running around me. What a fool!!! However, the time spent learning was not wasted as it gave me something 'feel good' and positive during a very negative time.

Whilst travelling in 2011, we were learning new things every day; our minds were being opened. I felt excited by the new skills I was learning in cooking classes, brainier with every museum we visited and more confident with all the interesting people we met. This is when I realised learning something new is a valuable Tool that had helped me rebuild my self-esteem and allowed me to focus my energies more positively during stressful times. On returning home, I firmly placed this Tool in My Wellness Toolbox and committed to using it with force at least once a year.

At the beginning of 2013, during the run-up to our wedding, I found myself returning home from work most nights with headaches or in tears; I was finding the unexpected content of the contract role very stressful and it was not helped by the growing list of all things 'Wedding' and the random demands and judgements left, right and centre. I was tired, feeling constantly run down and I was starting to feel negative. I was forgetting to use my Tools.

So, My Wellness Toolbox was opened and Tool #20 was dusted off. Time to take back some control. I did some research and booked myself on to a wine tasting course. It did not lead to the immediate career change I was plotting (an unexpected pregnancy a few months later put that idea to one side) but this would provide me with three days over a three-week period where I changed the subject. I did something I enjoyed. I had ME time. I had a break from the office. I met new people, positive people who I laughed with. On those three days I didn't get the train to work to face stressful phone calls about IT problems, I got the train to the wine-tasting school where it was acceptable to sip beautiful wines at 10 o'clock in the morning. It also led to me walking away with a Level 2 Award in Wines & Spirits, or, as I like to put it, "I'm a qualified wine taster". It made me happy and had helped put me back on the positive track. Tick.

In 2014, when pregnant with my first child, I was introduced to Tool #17 – Reiki. Amazed yet puzzled by the positive benefits Reiki had on my wellbeing, I wanted to learn more. In 2016, I found myself seven months pregnant with Baby No. 2 sitting on a Reiki Level 1 training course learning how to self-heal. I met some really interesting and inspiring people that weekend, so many amazing stories and experiences were shared, it was emotional yet uplifting. The nature of the course meant I left feeling relaxed and recharged with the added bonus that I was able to self-heal. Crying with happiness on the way home, I was quite taken aback by how emotional the sense of achievement had made me. I needed it. Little did I know then that this was just the start of an incredible, life-changing, educational journey.

The birth of our daughter brought so much happiness and loveliness to our lives, resulting in amazing times in 2017. However, at times, that year had been tough going as we dealt with grief and other stressful life events. It was no surprise that towards the end of the year, when my daughter was ten months old, I was frantically searching amongst my Tools and decided to pull this out once more to bring some new focus.

A few weeks later and I was sitting on a Reiki Level 2 training course expanding my knowledge further and learning how to heal others. I am a strong believer that everything happens for a reason. It was on this training course that I was able to take a step back and reflect on the year gone by, let go of some of the events (and difficult people…) and regain perspective. This learning malarkey is so good for that. Once again leaving with a huge sense of achievement, my self-esteem was gradually lifting higher and higher.

Learning something new can snowball. At the start of 2018, I made the decision to work towards qualifying as a Reiki practitioner… a student once more, surrounded by books and training courses, my mind expanding daily, spending time with so many influential and positive people, leading me to a wealth of exciting opportunities, motivating me to work extremely hard; so much that I qualified in March 2018.

The content of what I am doing leads me to automatically use Tool #9 – Daily Self-Care and, most importantly, help others, which is the main driver and very rewarding. Something I showed interest in four years ago is now becoming part of a new career. Smiling.

You never know where learning something new may take you… or to who?!?!

Effectiveness: 9/10. This Tool can be super effective in helping your mind grow and allowing you to refocus.

Ease: It really depends on what you choose to learn. Just be careful not to put too much pressure on yourself, especially if what you want to learn requires you to take on extra study alongside work and family. Be realistic and enjoy.

Budget: This is completely down to you, your budget, and what and how you want to learn. I have been pleasantly surprised by the offers you can get, especially for online training courses. Do some research and it may expand your possibilities even further.

"Live as if you were to die tomorrow.
Learn as if you were to live forever."
(Mahatma Ghandi)

TOOL #21
KINDNESS

The great thing about Tool #21 – Kindness is that it not only has a direct benefit on your health and happiness, but it has the same positive impacts on those that receive your kindness. It has been scientifically proven that kindness is good for the hearts and immune systems of all involved. This is one magic Tool that works brilliantly alongside Tool #15 – Gratitude and also makes you a positive person (Tool #14) for someone else.

In 2006 I struggled to think of one positive thing about myself, but today, if I was to write down my positive personality traits, I am confident kindness is high up on that list. At least once a week I ensure I go out of my way to perform a random act of kindness. It raises a smile very easily and not just for me.

Try one or two of these today and watch the magic of kindness unfold with immediate effect:

- Send a random text to a friend or family member to check how they are doing
- Give everyone your smile
- Unexpectedly buy lunch for your friend when the bill arrives
- If you see anyone struggling to open or navigate through a door, go out of your way to help
- Send flowers to a loved one for no reason
- Ask a stranger how they are
- When going through the checkout, let the person behind you go first
- Give something away for free instead of selling it on eBay (or similar)
- Do a chore/task for someone as a surprise
- If you see a stranger is upset, go and offer them a smile... or even a hug
- Give up your seat on the train/bus to a stranger
- Post a card to someone to let them know you are thinking about them
- If you see a parent struggling with an upset child go and ask if they are OK
- Give a colleague, who you know walks or gets the bus, a lift home
- Offer to pay for the shopping of the person in front of you at the till
- When you see the postman or the bin men, pop out and say thank you for the job they do

- Send a surprise gift to someone
- Ask a homeless person if there is anything they need and go and get it for them
- Double the tip you would normally give to the waiting staff in a bar or restaurant
- Compliment someone everyday
- Leave a lovely note for a loved one to find when they least expect it
- When popping to the shop, ask your neighbour if they need anything
- Keep a spare umbrella in the car and give it away when you are driving along and see someone walking without one in the pouring rain
- Volunteer for a local charity event
- Pick up litter when you spot it
- Buy a lottery ticket and give it to a stranger
- Help someone who may need assistance cross the road safely
- When buying your morning caffeine hit, buy one for the stranger in front of you
- Donate and deliver books in good condition to hospitals and charities
- Buy a friend a spa/beauty treatment as a random gift

Kindness has an incredible ripple effect; once it starts the kindness keeps moving along from person to person. It feels especially good when you know you are the one that started the chain.

I also think being kind to others sets a good example for our children. Before my eldest turned three, we were buying some chocolate treats. On the way into the shop I had acknowledged a homeless guy sitting outside. I asked my son to choose a chocolate bar for him, explaining that the chocolate may make the man smile. As we left the shop I encouraged my son to hand over the chocolate bar himself. Next to the guy was a dog and my son independently said the sweetest thing: "This is for you, but you must give some to the doggy too… OK?!". I will never forget how it made that man and the woman walking alongside us smile. Kindness makes you and others feel so good.

Finally, do not forget Tool #9 – Self-Care and be kind to yourself too. Every day.

Effectiveness: 10/10. Kindness makes you feel good every time.

Ease: 10/10. The ability to be kind is in all of us; you choose to be kind, it is that easy.

Budget: Free–£depends… that is up to you depending on your act of kindness.

"I've been searching for ways to heal myself, and I've found that kindness is the best way."

(Lady Gaga)

TOOL #22
PHYSICAL EXERCISE

We all know that physical exercise is good for you and can have amazing results for your wellbeing. It is known to relieve stress and anxiety, improve memory and sleep patterns, boost overall mood and can even increase your sex drive.

Yet I must admit this is probably the most unused Tool in My Wellness Toolbox, which is a shame because when I go through my moments of motivation (assuming they occur when I have the time) to exercise, I really enjoy the buzz it gives me, and I always realise the benefits quickly, both physically and emotionally.

The thing is, I also really enjoy evenings cuddling into my sofa under a blanket, sipping on a glass of chilled wine, and that option seems to win a lot, especially during the colder months. I know both are good for me (in moderation), so it is about finding the balance to do both... which I am still working on... again... but I am getting better... and will always keep hold of this Tool as I know how important it is!

Just a few exercise suggestions that have worked for me over the years...

Walking & Talking

Walking and talking with a good friend does not feel like exercise, yet those miles will clock up as you put the world to right and have a good release of everything and anything. Good for the body and mind and even better if there is a pub at the end of the walk!!

Team Sport/Netball

In the early noughties, when I was really struggling with anxiety, I joined the company netball team. This was a wonderful thing to do. For the time I was on that court, whether training or playing, I had to focus on the game, work as part of a team and get the endorphins pumping, and it enabled me to switch off from the negative thinking, even if it was just for an hour on that day. I always ached like hell the following day, but I loved it.

Ironically, it was a couple of years later when the anxiety had taken a full-on grip that I started managing the team. It then became quite a stressful thing for me do to. I made the decision to step away completely and I have not played since. A complete shame but a valuable lesson learned: know your limits! If you love something and it works for you, don't change it to please others.

Dance Exercise

In 2015, Zumba, a Colombian dance exercise, was introduced to me by my lovely friend. I was very motivated to join the Zumba class as I was eager to shift the post-pregnancy weight (aka new baby, convenient takeaway indulgence) that was still lingering. It was great fun and generated lots of giggles, possibly because I was so bad at it. Zumba did not feel like hard work even if I was losing my breath by the end of every routine; it is an enjoyable calorie burner. The music is uplifting and I was also surrounded by Tool #14 – Positive People. Zumba was very good for me. Parental responsibilities, logistics and, no doubt, an ounce of laziness meant I stopped going to the class. Cue rolling eyes.

Recently I came across an advert for cha-samba, a new dance fitness class being held in the village hall over the road from where I live, it is on a day that suits and does not clash with any other responsibilities at that time… and is pay as you go. No wasted cash. No excuses. All boxes ticked. It is BRILLIANT. The music blasts as we 'attempt' jive, cha-cha, samba and bhangra routines. It is energising and very uplifting, a great mood booster and good for the soul. We dance like no one is watching… because no one is… they are looking at their own feet. Another lesson learned – when choosing exercises, make sure they tick all the requirement boxes (location, content, cost) as you are more likely to stick to them.

Which leads me nicely on to my relationship with the gym.

The Gym & Personal Training

I have had more gym memberships over the years than I have fingers and toes. I have wasted a lot of money and that would always make me feel guilty. So, in 2015 I decided to finally step away from the gym relationship that was becoming a negative cycle for me. I stopped pretending that "This time would be the time I would embrace and enjoy it", "I may not use the actual gym, but I will go to all the classes", "I will use the pool even though I hate coming outside in the cold with wet hair"… blah…blah…blah.

I stopped making myself feel guilty for not going. I stopped doing something that I didn't enjoy. Do not get me wrong – I am not slagging off gyms, they are wonderful places for physical activity and I get why some people love them, but I finally accepted that I am not one of those people… and that's OK. However, something I did find quite useful at the gym was the personal training service that I used in the run-up to my wedding in 2013.

I found the personal trainer made my gym experience more sociable, I was guided to use equipment correctly and having someone shouting down my ear "Work harder… run faster" and "You can't be sick running at that speed on the spot" was what I needed to push me harder to fit into my wedding dress. However, the cost of membership plus the cost of the personal trainer was not sustainable, so as soon as I waved goodbye to the PT, that gym relationship also failed.

That is why, in 2015, post-pregnancy and after another failed gym relationship, I knew I had to increase my physical activity once more but found it hard to escape the house with a small child. I loved walking, but it wasn't having the desired effect on my waistline, which was demotivating.

I researched and found a home-based personal trainer. Darran rocks up at your own home, at agreed times, for one hour of hardcore physical exercise to boost the mood and completely knacker you out. There is no journey there and no journey back, i.e. there are no options for a detour to the pub, but it does mean I do not have to worry about sorting childcare. Sometimes it hurts, sometimes it makes me feel sick, sometimes I do not want to answer that door (especially when I see the blanket looking lonely on the sofa) but no matter how tired I am at the start, I always feel lifted (and very sweaty) at the end of a session. My fitness levels have improved vastly, exercise really is good for me. I have never wasted money having a personal training session so there is no guilt like the gym gave me; it is an investment in me and my wellbeing. Excellent value.

Writing this has made me reflect on how good the physical exercise Tool is and how I should try and utilise it a lot more. So this evening, as I sit with my feet up and snuggle into my sofa, I may just put on my Davina Fit in Five DVD to make sure I don't forget…

Effectiveness: 9/10. When I use this Tool it is very effective and really does me the world of good. I just need to realise it more.

Ease: ?/10. It depends on you and your relationship with exercise. This score changes weekly for me.

Budget: Exercise can be as cheap or as expensive as you want to make it. Do some research and find the right exercise for you that doesn't break your bank and that you can commit to. You may be surprised by what you can get for your money – especially if you currently have a gym membership you don't use!!

TOOL #23
LAUGHTER

Laughter really is a great medicine for mind and body; that is why this Tool is one of the firm favourites in My Wellness Toolbox and I search for laughter every day. It is also contagious, so when you start laughing you pass it on and make others feel good too.

The benefits of laughing and smiling are endless. They boost both mood and immunity at the same time, lower stress hormones, ease anxiety and tension, relieve stress, strengthen resilience, help defuse conflict, relax muscles from head to toe, increase energy... BURN CALORIES... and all of this for free.

I remember sitting in my first cognitive behavioural therapy session and explaining that I felt like a fraud, that my smile was often fake and my laughter forced, that I often used humour to try and cover my real feelings. The therapist said, "Why is that a problem?"

She explained that every time I laughed and smiled my body did not know it was fake; it received the surge of positivity as my brain released the endorphins. Laughing stops distressing emotions in their tracks, you can't feel anxious when you are laughing. Even if it felt fake, it was doing me good. She said, "The more you do it, the better you will feel, that smile will feel real again, fake it until you make it." She wasn't wrong.

The reality is that some days you do not feel like laughing. A sense of humour failure (for all the right reasons) may have become the norm, so you have to search for it and maybe just start with an extra few smiles a day. Here are some ideas:

- If you hear somebody else laughing, smile knowing that someone else is feeling good.
- Pull out Tool #15 – Gratitude and write down ten things you are grateful for. Just thinking about the good things in your life will help you smile.
- Think about something that made you laugh and replay it in your head, write it down or tell someone else about it.
- Seek out Tool #14 – Positive People, the ones that make you laugh. There is a comedian in all our lives; they have the ability to find humour in everything and love making others smile.
- Do an activity that makes you feel good.
- Watch your favourite comedy movie or TV show.

- Watch a comedian on YouTube… one minute with Michael McIntyre and I'm normally howling.
- Play a game with children. Their smiles and laughter are contagious, and they are the experts at it…
- Think about your most embarrassing moment and dare to share it. Laughing at yourself makes life less serious.
- Read a joke book. Even the bad dad jokes will curve the lips upwards.
- Do something silly.
- Look through photo albums and be grateful for all the good times you have experienced.
- Google funny quotes.
- When walking along the street, put your phone away, lift your head and smile at everyone you pass.
- Look for the humour in a difficult situation rather than focusing on all the negatives.

Just one week after our daughter was born, my husband's father fell very ill and came to live with us. Four months later to the day she was born, he would sadly pass away. It was a challenging and very sad time, yet during that time we all, including my father-in-law, found some humour in the experience of living under the same roof. I think some friends found it odd, maybe even cold, that we would chuckle as we relayed some of the experiences and conversations we had during what was a very sad and tough time. Yet those moments of humour kept us going and are now very fond memories that we can treasure. Laughter can help you grieve and bring you closer together.

Effectiveness: 10/10. Laughter really is the best medicine...

Ease: 8/10. Some days it can be hard to raise a smile so extra effort is required...

Budget: Laughter should cost you nothing!!

"Always find a reason to laugh. It may not add years to your life but it will surely add life to your years."

(Unknown)

TOOL #24
HYPNOBIRTHING

As I recall, from about the age of 25 it felt like I was constantly being asked, "So when do you think you will have children?" regardless of my relationship status. In the run-up to our wedding when I was 33, the question was slightly reworded… "So how long after you are married do you think you will have children?" Give me a chance to put my garter on!!!

Not only did I find this question annoying, it can be insensitive (and I have to hold my hands up as I am sure these words have spilled from my own mouth during small talk). I don't think I ever gave two people the same answer. Truth is, I didn't know the answer myself.

Do I actually want to have children? Can I have children? When is the right time for children? Am I really too old? Will I have a safe pregnancy? Will pregnancy bring the anxiety back? What if I have a panic attack during labour? What if I have to go to a hospital? Is anxiety genetic? Is it wrong I have not had children yet? What if I am not maternal? You get the gist…

The pressure people put on you when you haven't popped a baby out by a certain age is just that, pressure. Asking someone with a history of anxiety, what you think is a simple question can be a trigger to a series of questions in their inner head that can lead to negative thought patterns and panic.

It was not until our honeymoon that my husband and I agreed that the next step for us would be a family. We also agreed no pressure, we would relax things and see what would happen over the next 12 months. Therefore, we were pleasantly shocked and incredibly grateful when a few weeks after returning from our honeymoon I would discover we were pregnant. Delighted. Then all those unanswered irrational questions started to tumble through my head… It was time to be proactive and find a Tool to prevent the worry turning into reality.

Introducing the answer… Tool #24 – Hypnobirthing.

Hypnobirthing provides pregnant ladies with the Tools, including self-hypnosis, relaxation and breathing techniques, to help them towards having a calm and relaxed birth experience. For me it was so much more.

After the first group class I had let go of my fear of hospitals; there was not an ounce of anxiety when I went for my next appointment. Unbelievable. This was not just having a benefit on my pregnancy and the birth of my firstborn, this was removing deep-rooted fears that were still hanging around from years gone by.

During the classes we were able to meet fellow parents-to-be and could openly voice the anxieties and concerns we had about pregnancy and parenthood. Sharing is often releasing. The fear release activities (see also Tool #16 – Let Go & Release Techniques) enabled us to 'neutralise' the fears through discussion and then replace them with a positive affirmation. Tool #11 – Affirmations was effectively used daily throughout my pregnancy.

The hypnosis CD provided, which included relaxing music (Tool #3 pops up again), not only helped me relax and drift into a deep sleep but became a regular request from my husband who found it really soothing after a hard day in the office.

The ongoing guidance and reassurance from Liz, our lovely hypnobirthing teacher, was so instrumental in keeping me calm, especially in the last few weeks when the estimate date came and went, and my impatience kicked in.

Then after two days of surges, when the birth plan went flying out the window at full speed, all the Tools we had been given became even more paramount. I hadn't slept for over 36 hours yet I remained calm, focused and confident that my baby would arrive safely. Tools were flying everywhere, working hard for me and my husband and, most importantly, my baby boy.

Then my boy arrived. A calm, settled, smiley, hypnobirthing baby.

I was now a mummy and I would quickly be

introduced to the motherhood emotional curveballs that the role brings. The self-hypnosis CD, the music, the breathing exercises, the fear releases, all the specific Tools that hypnobirthing provided, would continue to be used forevermore.

When I fell pregnant for the second time, I was quite amazed by how many people congratulated us and within minutes would ask, "So do you think you will have a C-section again?" or how many times during my pregnancy others would provide their opinion or ask what decision I had made: "VBAC or C-section?". It felt like I was under pressure to decide and it was making me anxious. What was the right thing to do? Who knew? I just wanted my baby to arrive safely. I prepared for both. C-section booked in, with option to opt out at any-time, including on the date.

My baby boy had arrived by emergency C-section. Even though it wasn't the hypnobirthing water birth I envisaged, even when blue lights and emergency buttons were involved, I remained calm throughout. I knew that was down to all the hypnobirthing Tools. Therefore, this time, regardless of what decision I or the baby made about how they would arrive, hypnobirthing classes were a no-brainer and we booked in once more with the lovely Liz.

Closer to the birth, my husband and I made the joint decision that we would let the dates decide: if baby had not arrived by the planned C-section date, we would go ahead with it.

We arrived at the hospital. Waddling over the car park, my husband and I reflected about how different this experience was from the last – turning up in the family car was not quite the same as arriving beneath blue flashing lights. There was no quick entry on a trolley today, yet I still felt tremendously nervous. I focused on my affirmations, trusting my decisions. We met the other parents 'booked in' and shared our stories (and now friendships). I felt at ease before we were taken to the pre-op ward for initial assessment.

I remained focused as we waddled down to the operating theatre, then we had to wait outside for five minutes and I felt the nerves kicking in once more. The breathing exercises automatically kicked in and I continued to use them on the operating table until I heard the midwife gasp. I will never forget that gasp. Then I heard a cry. My baby's cry. With tears in her eyes, the midwife announced, "You have a daughter." My husband and I both burst into tears of pure joy. My beautiful calm girl was placed next to me and once again my life changed forever.

There were a few unexpected delays during the operation to put me back together, so Daddy and daughter were taken away for cuddles. Yet even during those 20 minutes of uncertainty and just wanting to be with my new baby, I remained calm, continuing to use my hypnobirthing Tools.

I chose hypnobirthing to be proactive. I was concerned that this life-changing event could bring back anxiety, so I did something about it. I did not cross my fingers and hope all would be OK, I took a positive step to influence the outcome.

The added bonus is that hypnobirthing is not just about preparing you for a positive birth. The new Tools I gained and the existing ones I enhanced will continue to be used for motherhood, other major life-changing events and beyond.

Effectiveness: 10/10. The most effective thing I could have chosen to do for me and my baby to keep anxiety away.

Ease: 8/10. Effort is required to decide how you want to learn and attend hypnobirthing (self-taught, MP3, books, online, group classes, private sessions etc), then you will most likely be required to practise affirmations, listen to music and self-hypnosis CDs etc, which becomes easier the more you do it. So worth it.

Budget: This really does depend on how you want to learn hypnobirthing. If you have a small budget, it can be self-taught (with books and MP3s). We personally wanted to attend group classes with a qualified hypnobirthing professional. The classes we attended currently cost approx. £250 per couple for the course, including all materials and ongoing unlimited support until baby arrives. Private sessions cost approx. £400 for the course; these can be more flexible and tailored to the couple, provide one-to-couple teaching and all materials and ongoing unlimited support.

TOOL #25
WRITING

It was only whilst writing *My Wellness Toolbox* that I really appreciated what a valuable Tool writing is and how over more recent years this Tool has repeatedly contributed towards making me feel good, enabling me to express myself and encouraging me to release the serious stuff and let go.

As a teenager, writing was one of my favourite hobbies, especially creating poems and short stories. Even my A level choices were based on my love of writing and plan to be a journalist. That plan did not transpire and instead of heading off to university to study journalism, I found myself working 9–5 on an IT helpdesk. The writing dried up as technology absorbed all my energy and working life and other priorities took over. I stopped doing something I loved.

If only I knew during the darkest days that this was a Tool that could have lifted me out of the black hole sooner. I didn't – I can't change that now, but I can make sure I never let go of it in the future.

Writing is therapeutic and can be very effective in helping you through a healing process, especially if you are struggling to express your feelings through other forms of communication. These are just some of the ways I have used this Tool:

- You can write down the bad stuff – anxieties, fears. Rip them up and let them go. (See also Tool #16 for the WIDABI – Write It Down and Burn It Technique.)
- Writing down something that is upsetting you is a form of release allowing you to download. It can make the situation that is upsetting you seem clearer and easier to handle.
- If you are struggling to express how you feel to someone, write them a letter. You do not have to give them the letter but releasing the words can reduce and even remove some of the negative feelings you may be experiencing. This is especially useful when you have feelings of anger.
- Writing letters to heaven can help through the grieving process; it can bring a sense of closure. It can also encourage the tears that you are holding back to release. When my father-in-law passed away I felt an overwhelming sense of grief for our children. Writing a poem on behalf of them not only helped me grieve but they now have a lovely poem about their Grandad that they can read and share as they get older.

- When you wake at night and your head is in overdrive, write the thoughts or ideas down, park them and come back to them the next day knowing they won't be forgotten.
- When you are struggling to make a decision, writing down the pros and cons can give you some clarity, take away some of the confusion and make the decision process easier.
- Keeping a Gratitude Diary (see also Tool #15 – Gratitude) allows you to write down all the things you are grateful for. As you write them down you will immediately feel content and will no doubt be smiling.
- Spending some time writing funny poems and lovely words in friends' and family's birthday cards can be uplifting for you and them. It can also be a good use of Tool #23 – Laughter.
- Writing a journal, a diary, a story…

Writing *My Wellness Toolbox* has been so good for my mind, boosted my confidence and enabled me to really appreciate how far I have come in 12 years. Just knowing that I have helped one or two others by sharing My Wellness Toolbox has been so rewarding and is the real motivation behind every chapter. Writing continues to heal.

Effectiveness: 9/10. Writing is very effective in boosting your mood; it helps express and release unwanted thoughts and reduce stress levels.

Ease: 7/10. For me, time and writer's block can be the blockers that can make using this Tool difficult. Yet when you put your mind to it, find the time and the pen starts flowing, it will be hard to stop...

Budget: Free–£5 (the cost of a notebook and a pen that won't leak).

TOOL #26
ME (YOU)

There is one Tool in My Wellness Toolbox that keeps all the other Tools charged. Me.

When building your Wellness Toolbox, don't forget the most powerful Tool. You.

In 2006, I avoided eye contact with myself in the mirror, so I did not have to watch myself thinking.

Today I can look in the mirror, straight in the eye and thank myself for giving me another chance.

The person I couldn't bear to look at is the same person who lifted me out of the black hole. Me.

When you find the value in yourself, your entire world will change.

"I do not want to take anything away from the support and patience I have had from my lovely family and friends… but ultimately I have turned my life around. It had to start with Me… if you need/want to change something it has to start with You. Please ask for help. Good Luck."

(Alison Swift, August 1st 2016 Facebook Post)

THE TOOLS IN MY WELLNESS TOOLBOX

What will you be adding to yours?

1. WATER ☐
2. BREATHE ☐
3. MUSIC ☐
4. MEDIA – TURN IT OFF ☐
5. ESSENTIAL OILS ☐
6. COGNITIVE BEHAVIOURAL THERAPY ☐
7. GRATITUDE VISION BOARD ☐
8. RESCUE REMEDY ☐
9. DAILY SELF-CARE ☐
10. ACCEPTANCE ☐
11. AFFIRMATIONS ☐
12. NO ☐
13. SELF-HELP BOOKS ☐
14. POSITIVE PEOPLE ☐
15. GRATITUDE ☐
16. LET GO & RELEASE TECHNIQUES ☐
17. REIKI ☐
18. *THE SECRET, THE POWER, THE MAGIC* ☐
19. MASSAGE THERAPIES ☐
20. LEARN SOMETHING NEW ☐
21. KINDNESS ☐
22. PHYSICAL EXERCISE ☐
23. LAUGHTER ☐
24. HYPNOBIRTHING ☐
25. WRITING ☐
26. ME (YOU) ☐

_____

_____

_____

_____

_____

_____

_____

_____

_____

_____

_____

_____

_____

_____

_____

_____

_____

_____

_____

_____

_____

_____

_____

_____
_____
_____
_____
_____
_____
_____
_____
_____
_____
_____
_____
_____
_____
_____
_____
_____
_____
_____
_____
_____
_____
_____
_____

_____

_____

_____

_____

_____

_____

_____

_____

_____

_____

_____

_____

_____

_____

_____

_____

_____

_____

_____

_____

_____

_____

_____

_____

_____

_____

_____

_____

_____

_____

_____

_____

_____

_____

_____

_____

_____

_____

_____

_____

_____

_____

_____

_____

_____

_____

_____

_____